PRIMARY ACCOUNTS OF ABOLITIONIST
BY
John Brown

- Interviews pp 1 →
- Instrument of Providence

PRIMARY ACCOUNTS OF JOHN BROWN, ABOLITIONIST

Published by Firework Press

New York City, NY

First published 1859

Copyright © Firework Press, 2015

All rights reserved

Except in the United States of America, this book is sold subject to the condition that it shall not, by way of trade or otherwise, be lent, re-sold, hired out, or otherwise circulated without the publisher's prior consent in any form of binding or cover other than that in which it is published and without a similar condition including this condition being imposed on the subsequent purchaser.

ABOUT FIREWORK PRESS

Firework Press prints and publishes the greatest books about American history ever written, including seminal works written by our nation's most influential figures.

INTRODUCTION

John Brown (May 9, 1800 – December 2, 1859) holds a unique place in American history, often viewed as a force for good and an evil man at the same time. Brown was a revolutionary abolitionist in the United States who became famous in his own time for practicing armed insurrection as a means to abolish slavery for good. He led the Pottawatomie Massacre during which five men were killed in 1856 in Bleeding Kansas and became notorious for his attempted raid at Harpers Ferry in 1859. For that, he was tried and executed for treason against the state of Virginia, murder, and conspiracy. Brown has been called "the most controversial of all 19th-century Americans."

Brown's attempt in 1859 to start a liberation movement among enslaved African Americans in Harpers Ferry, Virginia (now West Virginia) electrified the nation. He was tried for treason against the state of Virginia, the murder of five pro-slavery Southerners, and inciting a slave insurrection and was subsequently hanged. Southerners alleged that his rebellion was the tip of the abolitionist iceberg and represented the wishes of the Republican Party to end slavery. Historians agree that the Harpers Ferry raid in 1859 escalated tensions that, a year later, led to secession and the Civil War.

Brown was hardly apologetic about his attempted raid. During his trial, Brown addressed the court, "Had I interfered in the manner which I admit, and which I admit has been fairly proved (for I admire the truthfulness and candor of the greater portion of the witnesses who have testified in this case), had I so interfered in behalf of the rich, the powerful, the intelligent, the so-called great, or in behalf of any of their friends, either father, mother, brother, sister, wife, or children, or any of that class, and suffered and sacrificed what I have in this interference, it would have been all right; and every man in this court would have deemed it an act worthy of reward rather than punishment."

That speech, along with other words and interviews spoken by Brown during and after his trial and imprisonment are contained here in a collection of *Primary Accounts of John Brown*. Included are the last letters to his family, his last speech, his interview in prison, and the final note he wrote the day he was executed which predicted that slavery would only be abolished through the spilling of blood.

Interview with John Brown in Prison

Senator Mason: Can you tell us who furnished money for your expedition?

John Brown: I furnished most of it myself; I cannot implicate others. It is by my own folly that I have been taken. I could easily have saved myself from it, had I exercised my own better judgment rather than yielded to my feelings.

Mason: You mean if you had escaped immediately?

Brown: No. I had the means to make myself secure without any escape; but I allowed myself to be surrounded by a force by being too tardy. I should have gone away; but I had thirty odd prisoners, whose wives and daughters were in tears for their safety, and I felt for them. Besides, I wanted to allay the fears of those who believed we came here to burn and kill. For this reason I allowed the train to cross the bridge, and gave them full liberty to pass on. I did it only to spare the feelings of those passengers and their families, to allay the apprehensions that you had got here in your vicinity a band of men who had no regard for life and property, nor any feelings of humanity.

Mason: But you killed some people passing along the streets quietly.

Brown: Well, sir, if there was anything of that kind done, it was without my knowledge. Your own citizens who were my prisoners will tell you that every possible means was taken to prevent it. I did not allow my men to fire when there was danger of killing those we regarded as innocent persons, if I could help it. They will tell you that we allowed ourselves to be fired at repeatedly, and did not return it.

Bystander: That is not so. You killed an unarmed man at the corner of the house over there at the water-tank, and another besides.

Brown: See here, my friend; it is useless to dispute or contradict the report of your own neighbors who were my prisoners.

Mason: If you would tell me who sent you here, — who provided the means, — that would be information of some value.

Brown: I will answer freely and faithfully about what concerns myself, — I will answer anything I can with honor, — but not about others.

Mr. Vallandigham: (who had just entered): Mr. Brown, who sent you here?

Brown: No man sent me here; it was my own prompting and that of my Maker, or that of the Devil, — whichever you please to ascribe it to. I acknowledge no master in human form.

Vallandigham: Did you get up this expedition yourself?

Brown: I did.

Vallandigham: Did you get up this document that is called a Constitution?

Brown: I did. They are a constitution and ordinances of my own contriving and getting up.

Vallandigham: How long have you been engaged in this business?

Brown: From the breaking out of the difficulties in Kansas. Four of my sons had gone there to settle, and they invited me to go. I did no go there to settle, but because of the difficulties.

Mason: How many are there engaged with you in this movement?

Brown: Any questions that I can honorably answer I will, — not otherwise. So far as I am myself concerned, I have told everything truthfully. I value my word, sir.

Mason: What was your object in coming?

Brown: We came to free the slaves, and only that.

Volunteer: How many men, in all, had you?

Brown: I came to Virginia with eighteen men only, besides myself.

Volunteer: What in the world did you suppose you could do here in Virginia with that amount of men?

Brown: Young man, I do not wish to discuss that question here.

Volunteer: You could not do anything.

Brown: Well, perhaps your ideas and mine on military subjects would differ materially.

Mason: How do you justify your acts?

Brown: I think, my friend, you are guilty of a great wrong against God and humanity, — I say it without wishing to be offensive, — and it would be perfectly right for any one to interfere with you so far as to free those you wilfully and wickedly hold in bondage. I do not say this insultingly.

Mason: I understand that.

Brown: I think I did right, and that others will do right who interfere with you at any time and at all times. I hold that the Golden Rule, "Do unto others as ye would that others should do unto you," applies to al who would help others to gain their liberty.

Lieutenant Stuart: Don't you believe in the bible?

Brown: Certainly I do.

Mason: Did you consider this a military organization in this constitution? I have not yet read it.

Brown: I did in some sense. I wish you would give that paper close attention.

Mason: You consider yourself the commander-in-chief of these "provisional" military forces?

Brown: I was chosen, agreeably to the ordinance of a certain document, commander-in-chief of that force.

Mason: What wages did you offer?

Brown: None

Stuart: "The wages of sin is death."

Brown: I would not have made such a remark to you if you had been a prisoner, and wounded, in my hands.

A Bystander: Did you not promise a negro in Gettysburg twenty dollars a month?

Brown: I did not.

Mason: Does this talking annoy you?

Brown: Not in the least.

Vallandigham: Have you lived long in Ohio?

Brown: I went there in 1805. I lived in Summit County, which was then Portage County. My native place is Connecticut; my father lived there till 1805.

Vallandigham: Have you been in Portage County lately?

Brown: I was there in June last.

Vallandigham: When in Cleveland, did you attend the Fugitive Slave law Convention there?

Brown: No, I was there about the time of the sitting of the court to try the Oberlin rescuers. I spoke there publicly on that subject; on the Fugitive Slave law and my own rescue. Of course, as far as I had any influence at all, I was supposed to justify the Oberlin people for rescuing the slaves, because I have myself forcibly taken slaves from bondage. I was concerned in taking eleven slaves from Missouri to Canada last winter. I think I spoke in Cleveland before the Convention. I do not know that I had conversation with any of the Oberlin rescuers. I was sick part of the time I was in Ohio with the ague, in Ashtabula County.

Vallandigham: Did you see anything of Joshua B. Giddings there?

Brown: I did meet him.

Vallandigham: Did you converse with him?

Brown: I did. I would not tell you, of course, anything that that would implicate Mr. Giddings; but I certainly met with him and had conversations with him.

Vallandigham: About the rescue case?

Brown: Yes, I heard him express his opinions upon it very freely and frankly.

Vallandigham: Justifying it?

Brown: Yes, sir; I do not compromise him, certainly, in saying that.

Vallandigham: Will you answer this: Did you talk with Giddings about your expedition here?

Brown: No, I won't answer that; because a denial of it I would not make, and to make any affirmation of it I should be a great dunce.

Vallandigham: Have you had any correspondence with parties at the North on the subject of this movement?

Brown: I have had correspondence.

Bystander: Do you consider yourself an instrument in the hands of Providence?

Brown: I do.

Bystander: Upon what principle do you justify your acts?

Brown: Upon the Golden Rule. I pity the poor in bondage that have none to help them: that is why I am here; not to gratify any personal animosity, revenge or vindictive spirit. It is my sympathy with the oppressed and the wronged, that are as good as you and as precious in the sight of God.

Bystander: Certainly. But why take the slaves against their will?

Brown: I never did.

Bystander: You did in one instance, at least.

Stephens, the other wounded prisoner, here said, "You are right. In one case I know the negro wanted to go back."

Bystander: Where did you come from?

Stephens: I lived in Ashtabula County, Ohio.

Vallandigham: How recently did you leave Ashtabula County?

Stephens: Some months ago. I never resided there any length of time; have been through there.

Vallandigham: How far did you live from Jefferson?

Brown: Be cautious, Stephens, about any answers that would commit any friend. I would not answer that.

(**Stephens** turned partially over with a groan of pain, and was silent.)

Vallandigham: Who are your advisers in this movement?

Brown: I cannot answer that. I have numerous sympathizers throughout the entire North.

Vallandigham: In northern Ohio?

Brown: No more than anywhere else; in all the free states.

Vallandigham: But you are not personally acquainted in southern Ohio?

Brown: Not very much.

Bystander: Did you ever live in Washington City?

Brown: I did not. I want you to understand, gentlemen, and *(to the reporter of the "Herald")* you may report that, — I want you to understand that I respect the rights of the poores and weakest of colored people, oppressed by the slave system, just as much as I do those of the most wealthy and powerful. That is the idea that has moved me, and that alone. We expected no reward except the satisfaction of endeavoring to do for those in distress and greatly oppressed as we would be done by. The cry of distress of the oppressed is my reason, and the only thing that prompted me to come here.

Bystander: Why did you do it secretly?

Brown: Because I thought that necessary to success; no other reason.

Bystander: have you read Gerrit Smith's last letter?

Brown: What letter do you mean?

Bystander: The "New York Herald" of yesterday, in speaking of this affair, mentions a letter in this way: -

"Apropos of this exciting news, we recollect a very significant passage in one of Gerrit Smith's letters, published a month or two ago, in which he speaks of the folly of attempting to strike the shackles off the slaves by the force of moral suasion or legal agitation, and predicts that the next movement made in the direction of negro emancipation would be an insurrection in the South."

Brown: I have not seen the "New York herald" for some days past, but I presume, from your remark about the gist of the letter, that I should concur with it. I agree with Mr. Smith that moral suasion is hopeless. I don't think the people of the slave States will ever consider the subject of slavery in its true light till some other argument is resorted to than moral suasion.

Vallandigham: Did you expect a general rising of the slaves in case of your success?

Brown: No, sir; nor did I wish it. I expected to gather them up from time to time and set them free.

Vallandigham: Did you expect to hold possession here till then?

Brown: Well, I probably had quite a different idea. I do not know that I ought to reveal my plans. I am here a prisoner and wounded, because I foolishly allowed myself to be so. You overrate your strength in supposing I could have been taken if I had not allowed it. I was too tardy after commencing the open attack — in delaying my movements through Monday night, and up o the time I was attacked by Government troops. It was all occasioned by my desire to spare the feelings of my prisoners and their families and the community at large. I had no knowledge of the shooting of the negro Heywood.

Vallandigham: What time did you commence your organization in Canada?

Brown: That occurred about two years ago; in 1858.

Vallandigham: Who was the secretary?

Brown: That I would not tell if I recollected; but I do not recollect. I think the officers were elected in May, 1858. I may answer incorrectly, but not intentionally. My head is a little confused by wounds, and my memory obscure on dates, etc.

Dr. Biggs: Were you in the party at Dr. Kennedy's house?

Brown: I was head of that party. I occupied the house to mature my plans. I have not been in Baltimore to purchase caps.

Dr. Biggs: What was the number of men at Kennedy's?

Brown: I decline to answer that.

Dr. Biggs: Who lanced that woman's neck on the hill?

Brown: I did. I have sometimes practiced in surgery when I thought it a matter of humanity and necessity, and there was no one else to do it; but I have not studied surgery.

Dr. Biggs: It was done very well and scientifically. They have been very clever to the neighbors, I have been told, and we had no reason to suspect them, except that we could not understand their movements. They were represented as eight or nine persons; on Friday there were thirteen.

Brown: There were more than that.

Q: Where did you get arms?

Brown: I bought them.

Q: In what state?

Brown: That I will not state.

Q: How many guns?

Brown: Two hundred Sharpe's rifles and two hundred revolvers, — what is called the Massachusetts Arms Company's revolvers, a little under navy size.

Q: Why did you not take that swivel you left in the house?

Brown: I had no occasion for it. It as given to me a year or two ago.

Q: In Kansas?

Brown: No. I had nothing given to me in Kansas.

Q: By whom, and in what state?

Brown: I decline to answer. It is not properly a swivel; it is a very large rifle with a pivot. The ball is large than a musket ball; it is intended for a slug.

Reporter: I do not wish to annoy you; but if you have anything further you would like to say, I will report it.

Brown: I would have nothing to say, only that I claim to be here in carrying out a measure I believe perfectly justifiable, and not to act the part of an incendiary or a ruffian, but to aid those suffering great wrong. I wish to say, furthermore, that you had better — all you people at the South — prepare yourselves for a settlement of this question, that must come up for settlement sooner than you are prepared for it. The sooner you are prepared the better. You may dispose of me very easily, — I am nearly disposed by now; but this question is still to be settled, — this negro question I mean; the end of that is not yet. These wounds were inflicted upon me — both saber cuts on my head and bayonet stabs in different parts of my body — some minutes after I had ceased fighting and had consented to surrender, for the benefit of others, not for my own. I believe the major would not have been alive; I could have killed him just as easy as a mosquito when he came in, but I supposed he only came in to receive our surrender. There had been loud and long calls of "surrender" from us, — as loud as men can yell; but in the confusion and excitement I suppose we were not heard. I do not think the Major, or anyone, meant to butcher us after we had surrendered.

An officer: Why did you not surrender before the attack?

Brown: I did not think it was my duty or interest to do so. We assured the prisoners that we did not wish to harm them, and they should be set at liberty. I exercised my best judgment, not believing the people would wantonly sacrifice their own fellow-citizens, when we offered to let them go on condition of being allowed to change our position about a quarter of a mile. The prisoners agreed by a vote among themselves to pass across the bridge with us. We wanted them only as a sort of guarantee of our own safety, — that we should not be fired into. We took them, in the first place, as hostages and to keep them from doing any harm. We did kill some men in defending ourselves, but I saw no one fire except directly in self-defense. Our orders were strict not to harm anyone not in arms against us.

Q: Brown, suppose you had every nigger in the United States, what would you do with them?

Brown: Set them free.

Q: Your intention was to carry off and free them?

Brown: Not at all.

A Bystander: To set them free would sacrifice the life of every man in this community.

Brown: I do not think so.

Bystander: I know it. I think you are fanatical.

Brown: And I think you are fanatical. "Whom the god would destroy they first make mad," and you are mad.

Q: Was it only your object to free the negroes?

Brown: Absolutely our only object.

Q: But you demanded and took Colonel Washington' silver and watch?

Brown: Yes; we intended freely to appropriate the property of slaveholders to carry out our object. It was for that, and only that, and with no desire to enrich ourselves with any plunder whatever.

Bystander: Did you know Sherrod in Kansas? I understand you killed him.

Brown: I killed no man except in fair fight. I fought at Black Jack Point and at Osawatomie; and if I killed anybody, it was at one of these places.

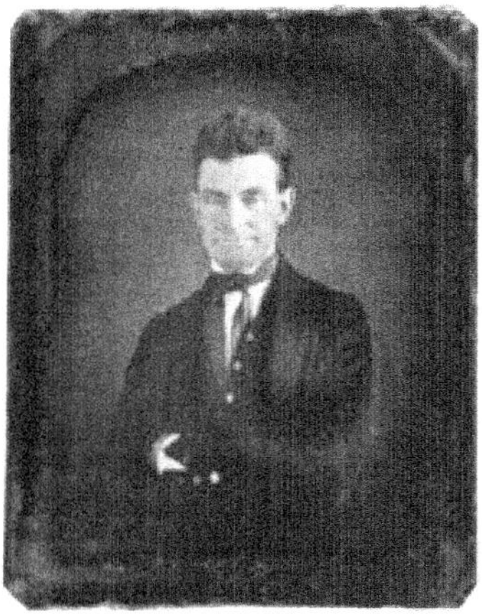

Letter from John Brown to His Family

Charles Town, Jefferson County, Va. October 31, 1859

My dear wife and children, every one,

I suppose you have learned before this by the newspapers that two weeks ago today we were fighting for our lives at Harpers Ferry; that during the fight Watson [one of Brown's sons] was mortally wounded, Oliver [another of Brown's sons] killed, William Thompson killed and Dauphin slightly wounded; that on the following day I was taken prisoner, immediately after which I received several saber-cuts on my head and bayonet-stabs in my body. As nearly as I can learn, Watson died of his wound on Wednesday, the second, — or on Thursday the third — the day after I was taken. Dauphin was killed when I was taken, and Anderson I suppose also. I have since been tried, and found guilty of treason, etc., and of murder in the first degree. I have not yet received my sentence. No others of the company with whom you were acquainted were, so far as I can learn, either killed or taken. Under all these terrible calamities, I feel quite cheerful in the assurance that God reigns and will overrule all for his glory and the best possible good. I feel no consciousness of guilt in the matter, nor even mortification on account of my imprisonment and irons; and I feel perfectly sure that very soon no member of my family will feel any possible disposition to "blush on my account." Already dear friends at a distance, with kindest sympathy, are cheering me with the assurance that posterity, at least, will do me justice. I shall command you all together, with my beloved but bereaved daughters-in-law, to their sympathies, which I do not doubt will soon reach you. I also commend you all to Him "whose mercy endureth forever," — to the God of my fathers, "whose I am, and whom I serve." "He will never leave you nor forsake you," unless you forsake Him. Finally, my dearly beloved, be of good comfort. Be sure to remember and follow my advice, and my example too, so far as it has been consistent with the holy religion of Jesus Christ, — in which I remain a most firm and humble believer. Never forget the poor, nor think anything you bestow on them to be lost on you, even though they may be black as Ebedmelech, the Ethiopian eunuch, who cared for Jeremiah in the pit of the dungeon; or as black as the one to who Philip preached Christ. Be sure to entertain strangers, for thereby some have — "Remember them that are in bonds as bound with them."

I am in charge of a jailer like the one who took charge of Paul and Silas; and you may rest assured that both kind hearts and kind faces are more or less about me, while thousands are thirsting for my blood. "These light afflictions, which are but for a moment, shall work out for us a far more exceeding and eternal weight of glory." I hope to be able to write to you again. Copy this, Ruth, [one of Brown's daughters] and send it to your sorrow-stricken brothers to comfort them. Write me a few words in regard to the welfare of all. God Almighty bless you all, and make you "joyful in the midst of all your tribulations!" Write to John Brown, Charles Town, Jefferson County, Va., care of Captain John avis.

Your affectionate husband and father,

John Brown

P.S. Yesterday, November 2, I was sentenced to be hanged on December 2 next. Do not grieve on my account. I am still quite cheerful. God bless you!

Yours ever,

Brown's Home

John Brown's Last Speech

I have, may it please the Court, a few words to say.

In the first place, I deny everything but what I have all along admitted, — the design on my part to free the slave. I intended certainly to have made a clean thing of the matter, as I did last winter, when I went into Missouri and there took slaves without the snapping of a gun on either side, moved them through the country, and finally left them in Canada. I designed to have done the same thing again, on a larger scale. That was all I intended. I never did intend murder, or treason, or the destruction of property, or to excite or incite slaves to rebellion or to make insurrection.

I have another objection; and that is, it is unjust that I should suffer such a penalty. Had I interfered in the manner which I admit, and which I admit has been fairly proved (for I admire the truthfulness and candor of the greater portion of the witnesses who have testified in this case), — had I so interfered in behalf of the rich, the powerful, the intelligent, the so-called great, or in behalf of any of their friends, — either father, mother, brother, sister, wife, or children, or any of that class, — and suffered and sacrificed what I have in this interference, it would have been all right; and every man in this court would have deemed it an act worthy of reward rather than punishment.

This court acknowledges, as I suppose, the validity of the law of God. I see a book kissed here which I suppose to be the bible, or at least the New Testament. That teaches me that all thing whatsoever I would that men should do to me, I should do even so to them. It teaches me further, to "remember them that are in bonds as bound with them." I endeavored to act upon that instruction. I say, I am yet too young to understand that God is any respecter of persons. I believe that to have interfered as I have done — as I have always freely admitted I have done — in behalf of his despised poor, was not wrong, but right. Now, if it is deemed necessary that I should forfeit my life for the furtherance of the ends of justice, and mingle my blood further with the blood of my children and with the blood of millions in this slave country whose rights are disregarded by wicked, cruel, and unjust enactments, — I submit; so let it be done!

Let me say one word further.

I feel entirely satisfied with the treatment I have received on my trial. Considering al the circumstances, it has been more generous than I expected. But I feel no consciousness of guilt. I have stated from the first what was my intention, and what was not. I never had any design against the life of any person, nor any disposition to commit treason, or excite slaves to rebel, or make any general insurrection. I never encouraged any man to do so, but always discouraged any idea of that kind.

Let me say, also, a word in regard to the statements made by some of those connected with me. I hear it has been stated by some of them that I have induced hem to join me. But the contrary is true. I do not say this to injure them, but as regretting their weakness. There is not one of them but joined me of his own accord, and the greater part of them at their own expense. A number of them I never saw, and never had a word of conversation with, till the day they came to me; and that was the purpose I have stated.

Now I have done.

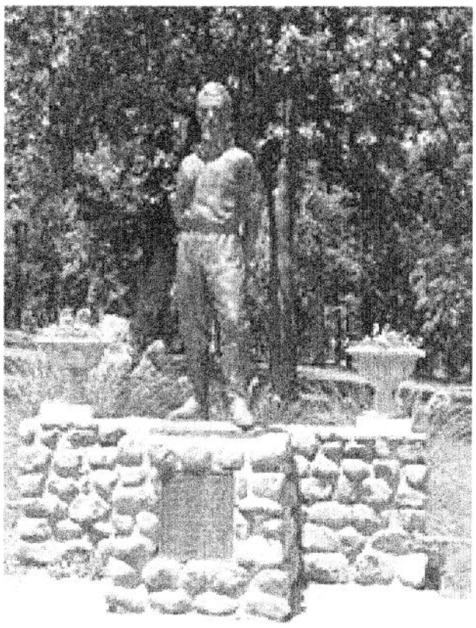

John Brown's Last Letter to His Family

Charles Town, Jefferson County, Va.
November 30, 1859

My dearly beloved wife, sons, and daughters, every one,

As I now begin probably what is the last letter I shall ever write to any of you, I conclude to write to all at the same time. I will mention some little matters particularly applicable to little property concerns in another place.

I recently received a letter from my wife, from near Philadelphia, dated November 22, by which it would seem that she was about giving up the idea of seeing me again. I had written her to come on if she felt equal to the undertaking, but I do not know that she will get my letter in time. It was on her own account, chiefly, that I asked her to stay back, but I do not know if she got my letter in time. It was on her own account, chiefly, that I asked her to stay back. At first I had a most strong desire to see her again, but their appeared to be very serious objections; and should we never meet in this life, I trust that she will in the need be satisfied it was for the best at least, if not most for her comfort.

I am waiting the hour of my public murder with great composure of mind and cheerfulness; feeling the strong assurance that in no other possible way could I be used to so much advantage to the cause of God and of humanity, and that nothing that either I or all my family have sacrificed or suffered will be lost. The reflection that a wise and merciful as well as just and holy God rules not only the affairs of this world but of all worlds, is a rock to set our feet upon under all circumstances, — even those more severely trying ones in which our own feelings and wrongs have placed us. I have now no doubt but that our seeming disaster will ultimately result in the most glorious success. So, my dear shattered and broken family, be of good cheer, and believe and trust in God with all your heart and with all your soul; for he doeth all things well. Do not feel ashamed on my account, nor for one moment despair of the cause or grow weary of well-doing. I bless God I never felt stronger confidence in the certain and near approach of a bright morning and glorious day that I have felt, and do now feel, since my confinement here. I am endeavoring to return, like a prodigal as I am, to my Father, against whom I have always sinned, in the hope that he may kindly and forgivingly meet me, though a very great way off.

Oh, my dear wife and children, would to God you could know how I have been travailing in birth for you all, that no one of you may fail of the grace of God through Jesus Christ; that no one of may fail of the grace of God through Jesus Christ; that no one of you may blind to the truth and glorious light of his Word, in which life and immortality are brought to light. I beseech you, every one, to make the Bible your daily and nightly study, with a child-like, honest, candid, teachable spirit of love and respect for your husband father. And I beseech the God of my fathers to open all your eyes to the discovery of the truth. You cannot imagine how much you may soon need the consolations of the Christian religion. Circumstances like my own for more than a month past have convinced me, beyond all doubt, of my own great need of some theories treasured up, when our prejudices are excited, our vanity worked up to the highest pitch. Oh, do not trust your eternal all upon the boisterous ocean, without even a helm or compass to aid you in steering! I do not ask of you to throw away your reason; I only ask you to make a candid, sober use of your reason.

My dear young children, will you listen to this last poor admonition of one who can only love you? Oh, be determined at once to give your whole heart to God, and let nothing alter or shake that resolution. You need have no fears of regretting it. Do not be vain and thoughtless, but sober-minded; and let me entreat you all to love the whole remnanat of our once great family. Try and build up again your broken walls, and to make the utmost of every stone that is left. Nothing can so tend to make life a blessing as the consciousness that your life and example bles and leave others stronger. Still, it is ground of the utmost comfort to my mind to know that so many of you as have had the opportunity have given some proof of your fidelity to the great family of men. Be faithful unto death; from the exercise of habitual love to man it cannot be very hard to love his Maker.

I must yet insert the reason for my firm belief in the divine inspiration of the bible, notwithstanding I am, perhaps, naturally skeptical, — certainly not credulous. I wish all to consider it most thoroughly when yo read that blessed book, and see whether you cannot discover such evidence yourselves. It is the putiry of heart, filling our minds as well as work and actions, which is everywhere insisted on, that distinguishes it from all other teachings, that commends it to my conscience. Whether my heart be willing and obedient or not, the inducement that it holds out is another reason of my conviction of its truth and genuineness; but I do not here omit this my last argument on the Bible, that eternal life is what my soul is panting for after this moment. I mention this as a reason for endeavoring to leave a valuable copy of the Bible, to be carefully preserved in remembrance of me, to so many of my posterity, instead of some other book at equal cost.

I beseech you all to live in habitual contentment with moderate circumstances and gains of worldly store, and earnestly to teach this to your children and children's children after you, by example as well as precept. Be determined to show by experience, as soon as may be, whether Bible instruction is of divine origin or not. Be sure to own no man anything, but to love one another. John Rogers wrote to his children: "Abhor the arrant whore of Rome." John Brown writes to his children to abhor, with undying hatred also, that sum of all villainies, — slavery. Remember, "he that is slow to anger is better than the mighty," and "he that ruleth his spirit that he that taketh a city." Remember also that "they being wise shall shine, and they that turn many to righteousness, as the stars for ever and ever."

And now, dearly beloved family, to God and the work of his grace I commend you all.

Your affectionate husband and father,
John Brown.

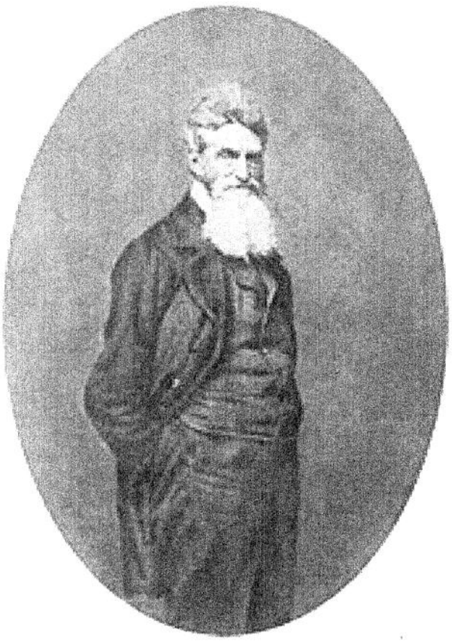

John Brown's Last Note on the Day of His Execution

Charlestown, Virginia Dec 2, 1859

I, John Brown, am now quite *certain* that the crimes of this *guilty land* will never be purged away but with *blood*. I had, as I now think vainly, flattered myself that without very much bloodshed it might be done.

Printed in Great Britain
by Amazon